The XXL Air Fryer Cookbook For Beginners

Delicious and Easy-Going Recipes For Every Day incl. Side Dishes, Snacks and Desserts

Holly M. Adams

ISBN - 9798840665794

2   **Holly M. Adams**

Table of Contents

Holly M. Adams

It's no secret that what we eat influences how we feel about not only ourselves, but the world around us. When we get plenty of rest and eat a balanced diet, we have more energy to do the things we love. We can focus more on our work and families and have more energy for pursuing our hobbies.

While this information is common knowledge for most of us, why is that we continually choose to consume food that we know will not help us much in the long run?

For example, many of us are aware that a diet heavy in fat can lead to increased health risks, yet supermarkets and restaurants are full of high-fat, calorie-laden foods. From deep-fried chicken to French fries submerged in fatty oils, Americans (overall) constantly choose fat-drenched foods. However, according to the National Health Service (NHS)[1], consuming high amounts of saturated fats potentially leads to increased LDL cholesterol. An increased level of LDL cholesterol puts you more at risk for both heart disease and stroke.

So what is it about fat-filled foods that make us want to eat them? In short, they taste good. The crispy, satisfying crunch of a well-cooked French fry or the hearty taste of a fried pork chop is enough to make us choose these meals again and again.

While, for most people, no harm comes from choosing a fattier meal every now and then, the problems begin to set in when fatty food becomes a lifestyle. Unfortunately, for a good portion of us, this same fatty food is also the most convenient, making it a significant reason for us to turn to these types of food throughout the week.

1 https://www.nhs.uk/live-well/eat-well/different-fats-nutrition/

On busy weeknights when the kids need help with homework and you're tired from a long day at the office, it's exceptionally easy to pop pre-fried fries into an oven. It's simple to fill the deep fryer with oil and dunk a couple of corn dogs in it for a few minutes.

But what if there was a way to have all of the convenience of fried food without the calories and health risks?

Fortunately, there is! Air fryers are a relatively new cooking appliance that has transformed kitchens around the world. Using minimal amounts of grease (if any), air fryers are a unique way to achieve delicious food in a short amount of time.

What is an Air Fryer?

Air fryers are somewhat similar to ovens, except they utilize heating elements that are located at the top of the device, rather than above and below. They have a fan that can disperse the heat rapidly through the interior of the air fryer, helping your food cook quickly and efficiently.

According to Good Housekeeping[2], deep fryers average around 10 minutes for their total heating time, compared to most air fryers which are able to heat almost instantaneously.

In terms of looks, air fryers are often relatively small and are completely enclosed when operating. They typically have a removable basket with a handle which is where you place the food, or a lid that opens, allowing you to place and remove food from the inner chamber.

---

2 https://www.goodhousekeeping.com/appliances/a28436830/what-is-an-air-fryer/

Benefits of Cooking with an Air Fryer

Using an air fryer to cook your food has a multitude of benefits over other devices. The compact size of the device makes it convenient for home chefs that have limited space in the kitchen.

As we mentioned, the most widely appreciated advantage of air frying is the limited amount of oil required. Some foods can be cooked without the addition of any oil at all, while others require just a tablespoon or so of oil to help the ingredients get crispy.

Less oil means fewer calories and less saturated fats, without compromising the texture of your food. While the food will taste differently due to less oil, it will be healthier and lighter.

Others enjoy using the air fryer thanks to the fact that most models can easily be disassembled and cleaned in the dishwasher. You won't have to worry about disposing large amounts of oil or cleaning up messy spills. Using an air fryer inside your home won't leave oily residue around the kitchen, so you'll spend even less time tidying up after your meal.

Perks of the air fryer also include less time spent monitoring your air fryer. While you'll want to always be in the same room as your fryer when it's in use, you can turn your attention to cooking another part of your meal while the air fryer is cooking. For example, if you've got chicken wings in the air fryer, you could be preparing a side salad at the same time to serve as part of your meal.

Another benefit of air fryers is their relatively low cost. Of course, the price varies between makes and models, but you can get a quality one for less than $75. Compared to some other cooking appliances, this cost isn't unreasonable, and many people find the price is overshadowed by the versatility of its cooking.

One last advantage of using an air fryer is that they are quick. In fact, you'll want to double check your air fryer's manual to ensure that you are following their recommended cooking times. Depending on how much food is in your fryer (specifically, how much space is available in the basket), your cooking times can change. You'll enjoy your meals faster with this handy appliance, so you can forget having to wait around on conventional ovens.

How to Choose the Right Air Fryer for You

The type of air fryer you need depends on a few different factors. Some things you'll want to consider before purchasing your appliance include:

- **Budget.** How much are you willing to spend on an air fryer? Do you plan to use it sparingly? If so, you may want to choose a cheaper one to start with. Are you 100% invested in frequently using your air fryer? It may be worth spending more to ensure you get the best quality and most value for your money.

- **Servings.** Consider how many people you typically cook for. Is it just you and one other person living in your home? A smaller air fryer will likely be the way to go, if so. However, if you have a larger family, you'll most likely want to purchase a larger one to ensure you can cook enough servings for your family at once to save you time.

- **Counter Space.** Most of us wish we had a bigger kitchen, especially when it comes to purchasing kitchen appliances. Do you have enough space for a large air fryer? What shape fryer will work well in your kitchen area? You'll want to know the measurements of your kitchen before buying one and determine where you will store your fryer.

Holly M. Adams

❧ **Wattage.** Check the wattage of each air fryer you are considering buying. You'll want to make sure the wattage is compatible with your kitchen's electrical setup. Some models may put too much stress on your electrical breakers, although this problem will likely only occur if you have several high-powered items operating at once.

Like with any purchases made in the modern era, you'll want to read reviews before purchasing your new air fryer. Check for any issues that customers have run into. If multiple people mention the same issue, you can bet you'll experience it at some point if you decide to purchase the item.

Each model will have its own pros and cons, so do your research to make sure you're investing in a purchase that will serve your needs well.

Things to Consider Before Purchasing

While most people consider air fryers a functional way to cook, there are a couple of things you will want to remember before you invest in air frying.

- **Variety.** You can only cook one type of food at a time in the air fryer. So if you're used to popping in multiple dishes in conventional ovens at the same time, you won't have that luxury with an air fryer.

- **Noise.** Air fryers use fans to help circulate the heat while cooking your meal. Be aware that these fans typically make noise, even when working properly. You can check reviews or manufacturer's information for any details about how loud the fan is.

- **No wet batter.** You'll want to stay away from very wet batter on foods, including wet-battered fried chicken. When you coat foods in a heavy batter, they often don't cook well in the air fryer as they would in another device.

- **Temperatures.** Most air fryers can only reach 400°F. While food will typically be cooked at lower temperatures than conventional ovens, you will still want to bear in mind that you won't be able to cook any food above the maximum temperature allowed on your particular model.

Holly M. Adams

Should you still buy an air fryer despite these considerations? That choice is ultimately up to you. One way to look at the situation is to determine how often you eat meals that are especially known for their heavy amounts of oil. If you find yourself eating fries or potato chips multiple times a week, you could very well find yourself saving hundreds of calories each week by switching over to air fryer cooking.

However, if you prefer salads with leafy greens, you may find that the air fryer doesn't necessarily get enough use in your particular kitchen to warrant the investment.

Safety Tips for Using Your Air Fryer

Even though you won't be using large amounts of oil in your air fryer, it's still important to monitor the device while it is in use. Don't assume that you can leave the air fryer for long periods of time. While the cooking time will be significantly reduced, you should actively check your food throughout the cooking process.

A few things safety tips to keep in mind while cooking with your air fryer:

- **Check your food often.** No one wants to eat a burned dinner. But burning food can present not just a bad meal but also a dangerous situation. Be sure to check your meal several times while cooking.

- **Keep your air fryer unplugged when not in use.** It's always a good idea to keep any appliance unplugged when you aren't using it. This habit prevents the device from unintentionally being activated.

- **Operate your air fryer away from water.** Of course, since your air fryer is electrically operated, you'll want to ensure you are not using it near any large amounts of water, especially while plugged in. Doing so can result in shock or electrocution. You'll want to be mindful of sink water and pitchers or glasses of water nearby while you're cooking.

❧ **Clean your air fryer frequently.** Keep your device free of crumbs, oil, and other build up. Allowing debris to build up over time can result in a fire hazard. Be sure to wash the basket and any trays according to instructions.

❧ **Use the appropriate tools.** Be sure you are using only approved accessories for your air fryer's particular make and model. Not using the right-shaped accessories or ones not intended for your device can lead to melted materials and improperly cooked foods.

❧ **Read the instruction manual.** Don't be tempted to just "wing" using an air fryer for the first few times. Read the manual that came with your fryer thoroughly before using. Save the manual in an easy-to-reach place so that you can consult it as necessary throughout your time in the kitchen.

Don't Cook These Foods in Your Air Fryer

Want to save yourself the disappointment of a poorly cooked meal? Be sure to avoid certain foods that are known to be less-than-perfect choices for air fryers.

While air fryers offer plenty of versatility in terms of food selection, there are some foods that are not suitable for cooking this way.

Examples include:

- Cheese

- Raw grains

- Fresh greens

- Foods with wet batter

- Popcorn

Getting to know what you can and can't cook in an air fryer will take a bit of practice. Keep in mind that you'll need to rethink your cooking process. Even the most experienced cooks will need to modify their routines slightly to get used to cooking with a new device.

Do a little research beforehand if you're not sure whether a certain food can go into the air fryer. If it's not mentioned in your manufacturer's manual, then do a quick online search. Chances are, someone else has tried cooking that exact food and has mentioned their experience with it. There are plenty of groups available online that are dedicated to helping new users understand how to better implement their air fryer recipes.

General Tips for Using Your Air Fryer

Fortunately, there are a few tips you can use to help you get acquainted with your air fryer more easily. As with using any new cooking appliance, it will take a bit of trial and error to learn how to cook the food just the way you prefer.

As always, we recommend consulting the manufacturer's manual, as this resource will have not only safety information but details about specific considerations for cooking.

Some points to remember when using any air fryer:

- **Use some oil.** Don't make the mistake of thinking you don't need to use any oil at all. While you obviously won't be using lots of it, applying a thin coat of oil on certain foods helps prevent them from drying out too much during the cooking process.

- **Flip food at least once.** Be sure to check your food while it cooks. Flipping the food at the halfway point will help ensure even cooking.

- **Don't overcrowd the basket.** Packing too much food in your basket will lead to soggy food and unevenly cooked pieces. Doing this could cause some parts of your food to be undercooked while other sections may begin to burn.

- ❧ **Plan some leeway time.** Experiment with cooking with your air fryer before cooking for others. Build in some time to play around with your recipes and device so that you aren't stressed when it comes time to cook for another person.

What Foods Cook Well in an Air Fryer?

While it may seem like there are a lot of limitations on what you can cook in the air fryer, there are plenty of items that you can cook without hesitation. Of course, it'll take a bit of getting used to in terms of learning more about your particular air fryer model as well as using less oil than normal.

Some of the foods that are known for cooking well in the air fryer include:

- Chicken wings

- French fries

- Vegetables

- Some breads

- Steak

- Bacon

Many of these foods are typically very messy to cook on the stove top, which makes using an air fryer even more convenient, as you'll spend less time cleaning up sticky messes. As we mentioned earlier, being able to just put the basket or tray into the dishwasher is ideal.

You can even experiment with your current recipes and adjust them for air fryer cooking. For example, you'll want to keep in mind that air fryers typically call for a lower temperature than traditional ovens, and depending on your exact model, your fryer could cook food much faster than you're used to. From appetizers to main courses, you're sure to find plenty of use for your air fryer if you invest a bit of time getting acquainted with using this new tool.

MAIN DISHES

||||||||||||||||||||||||||||||||||||||||||||||||||||||||||||||||||||||||||||||||||||

Perfectly Crisp Baked Potato with Toppings

Baked potatoes are an ideal meal for anyone that enjoys simplicity. Potatoes are easy to cook in the air fryer, and it's just as convenient to customize the toppings to suit your taste preferences. It's hard to beat baking potatoes in your air fryer when it comes to cooking a hearty meal that takes minimal effort yet is full on taste.

SERVES: 4

NUTRITION: FAT – 25G, NET CARBS – 33G, PROTEIN – 11.8G, CALORIES – 390

Ingredients:

- 4 baking potatoes (Russet, also known as "Idaho" potatoes)
- Olive oil spray (in a can)
- Salt and pepper
- 2 tbs. butter
- 1/4 lb. shredded cheddar cheese
- 1/2 cup of sour cream
- 1/4 cup of salsa

Holly M. Adams

1 Wash and dry each potato. Spray a bit of olive oil onto each potato and rub in as needed with your hands or a paper towel.

2 Place the potatoes in your air fryer's basket, making sure there is space between each of them. Depending on the size of your air fryer, you may be able to cook less or more potatoes at a time.

3 Cook the potatoes at 400°F for approximately 20 minutes. Open the basket and carefully flip the potatoes.

4 Cook an additional 20 minutes or until the potatoes are tender enough to prick with a fork.

5 Top each baked potato with ½ a tablespoon of butter. Salt and pepper as desired. Top with cheddar cheese, sour cream, and salsa.

Spicy Fried Chicken Drumsticks

Fried chicken doesn't have to be doused in large amounts of oil to be delicious. This spicy fried chicken recipe gives you the crispness you love without the extra calories. Be mindful of not adding too many of the breadcrumbs to your chicken, as using too many will make your chicken drier than desired.

SERVES: 4

NUTRITION: FAT – 9.2G, NET CARBS – 10.4G, PROTEIN – 10.7G, CALORIES – 168

Ingredients:

- 4 chicken legs (drumsticks)
- ½ cup of breadcrumbs
- 1 tsp. cayenne pepper
- ¼ tsp. garlic powder
- ¼ tsp. salt
- ¼ tsp. black pepper
- 1 egg (large)
- Olive oil spray (as necessary)

Method:

1 In a medium bowl, beat the egg well.

2 In another medium bowl, mix the breadcrumbs, cayenne pepper, garlic powder, salt, and black pepper.

3 Dry each chicken leg with a paper towel and then dunk into the beaten egg wash. Then roll the chicken leg in the breadcrumb mixture. Make sure you press in the breadcrumbs to keep them from falling off during the cooking process.

4 Put the chicken legs in the air fryer basket. Cook at 370°F for approximately 30 minutes. Check on the chicken at 10-minute intervals. If the chicken's coating looks too dry at any point, spray it with a pump or two of the olive oil spray to prevent it from burning.

5 Flip the chicken legs at least once during cooking to prevent the top part from burning.

6 Cook until the internal temperature of the chicken reaches 160°F, making sure your thermometer is not touching the bone when checking.

Flaky Cod Fillets with Lemon-Pepper Seasoning

Who doesn't love a delicious fillet of fried fish? The lemon-pepper seasoning in this recipe is the perfect blend of sour and peppery flavor. Lemon-pepper is a great choice for seasoning fish because these flavors do not overpower the light taste of the white fish. This recipe pairs well with air fryer-cooked French fries, adding up to a tasty fish and chips dinner!

SERVES: 3

NUTRITION: FAT – 5G, NET CARBS – 1.6G, PROTEIN – 10G, CALORIES – 90

Ingredients:

- 3 cod fillets (approx. 1/4 lb. each)
- 1/2 cup flour
- Avocado oil spray
- 2 fresh lemons
- 1 tbs. freshly cracked black pepper
- 1/2 tbs. garlic powder
- Salt
- Pepper

Method:

1. In a large bowl, mix the flour, black pepper, garlic powder, salt, and pepper.

2. Pat each cod fillet dry using a paper towel. Dunk each fillet in the flour mixture and cover the fish completely. Carefully shake off any excess flour. Use your hands to gently push the flour into the fish, to help prevent it from falling off during the cooking process.

3. Spray your air fryer's basket with some of the avocado oil. This step will help keep the fish fillets from sticking to the basket and losing their coating.

4. Cook at 350°F for approximately 15 minutes, flipping halfway through. Cook the fish until it reaches 145°F.

5. Serve fish with wedges of lemon.

Savory Mushroom-Swiss Burgers with Onions

Cooking burgers in your air fryer is easier than ever. You don't need to worry about greasing the fryer or adding any extra oils to the meat. You'll get evenly cooked burgers that are perfect each time. Note: For the juiciest burgers, you'll want to use 70% lean, but if you're wanting to limit the amount of fat in your diet, you can use 85% lean instead. Just be sure not to overcook them, or they may begin to dry out.

SERVES: 4

NUTRITION: FAT – 33.2G, NET CARBS – 33.6G, PROTEIN – 49.4G, CALORIES – 630

Ingredients:

- 1 lb. ground beef (see the note above)
- 4 hamburger buns
- 4 slices of Swiss cheese
- 1 basket of white button mushrooms
- 1 white onion
- ½ tbs. garlic powder
- 1 tbs. butter

1. Form 4, equal-sized patties from the hamburger meat. Make a small indentation with your thumb in each burger to help it cook evenly.

2. Place the burgers in the air fryer, spacing them out so they aren't touching. Cook at 375°F for approximately 10 minutes. Cook for about 5 minutes per side, flipping halfway through. Ensure the internal temperature reaches 160°F. Depending on the size of your air fryer, you may need to do two separate batches.

3. While the burgers cook, slice the onion into thin wedges, about 1/2-inch wide. Remove the stems from the mushrooms and slice the mushroom caps into 1/4-inch pieces.

4. Heat a tablespoon of butter in a large saucepan. Once the butter has melted, add the onions and mushrooms to the pan.

5. Sprinkle the garlic powder over the onions and mushrooms. Mix in and sauté for approximately 10 minutes, or until both ingredients are tender.

6 Toast the hamburger buns in a toaster. If your toaster isn't big enough to fit them, you can also toast them on a griddle a medium-high heat for two or three minutes.

7 Place the burgers on the buns. Top with a slice of Swiss cheese and the onions and mushrooms.

Honey-Garlic Salmon

Cooking any type of fish evenly can be difficult with traditional methods. The air fryer eliminates that problem, so long as you use even cuts of fish and allow for enough room for the air to circulate around the fish. Give this honey-garlic salmon recipe a try and enjoy the ease of cooking with an air fryer.

SERVES: 2

NUTRITION: FAT – 18G, NET CARBS – 37.4G, PROTEIN – 35.5G, CALORIES – 437

Ingredients:

- 🍽 2 salmon fillets
- 🍽 1 tbs. olive oil
- 🍽 ½ tsp. salt
- 🍽 ½ tsp. garlic powder
- 🍽 ½ tsp. black pepper
- 🍽 2 cloves minced garlic
- 🍽 ¼ cup of honey
- 🍽 1 tbs. soy sauce

1 Pat the salmon fillets dry with a paper towel. Drizzle the tablespoon of olive oil over them and spread out the oil to make sure the entire fillet is covered both on the skin side and the top side.

2 In a small bowl, mix together the salt, garlic powder, and black pepper. Sprinkle this seasoning onto the side of the salmon without the skin. Lightly push in the seasonings to help them adhere to the fish's surface.

3 Place the salmon fillets on your air fryer tray with the skin side touching the tray. Depending on the size of the fillets, you may have to do these in two separate batches.

4 Cook at 400°F for approximately 6 minutes.

5 While the salmon cooks, mix the honey, minced garlic, and soy sauce together in a small bowl.

6 After the 6 minutes are up, pull out the tray and drizzle the honey mixture over the tops of the salmon. Cook for an additional two minutes to allow the honey to thicken and the garlic to become slightly browned.

Buffalo Chicken Wings

Chicken wings are the perfect dish to make when you're having guests over. You can make these wings in batches, popping them in and out of the air fryer easily. Having the sauce on hand for after they cook makes this step even simpler. Another plus of adding the sauce at the end means that people can decide how spicy they want their wings.

SERVES: 4

NUTRITION: FAT – 40.4G, NET CARBS – 1G, PROTEIN – 66G, CALORIES – 643

Ingredients:

- 2 lbs. chicken wings (with bones and skin)
- 1.5 tbs. avocado oil
- 1/2 tsp. garlic powder
- 1/4 tsp. cayenne pepper
- 1/4 tsp. chipotle pepper
- 1/2 tsp. onion powder
- 1/4 tsp. salt
- 1/4 tsp. black pepper
- 1 stick of butter (salted)
- 2 cups of vinegar-based hot sauce

1 Lay the chicken wings in a large bowl. Pour the avocado oil over the wings and use tongs or two spoons to toss the wings in the oil.

2 In a small bowl, mix together the garlic powder, onion powder, cayenne pepper, chipotle pepper, salt, and black pepper. Sprinkle the seasoning on the wings and toss again to make sure the mixture gets on all of the wings.

3 Place the wings on your air fryer's tray and cook at 370°F for about 20 minutes, flipping them over around the 10-minute mark.

4 While the wings are cooking, prepare the sauce. Melt the stick of butter over low heat on the stove top.

5 Add the two cups of hot sauce and mix well. You can adjust the level of spiciness by adding or reducing the amount of hot sauce.

6 Once the chicken wings have reached an internal temperature of 165°F, remove them from the air fryer. Serve as is or toss with the hot sauce. Alternately, you can serve the wings with the sauce on the side, allowing your guests to add as much or as little hot sauce as they like.

Black-Pepper Seasoned, Marinated Steak

Steak cooked in an air fryer? It's true. Cooking meat in your fryer is a luxury, especially in terms of clean up time. Steak is a notoriously messy dish to cook on the stovetop, and making it in the air fryer helps contain the mess to one convenient location. Additionally, it's easier to get an even cook throughout your steak when you cook it with the circulating warm arm. This recipe can easily be doubled if you want to make enough marinade for another steak. Keep in mind you'll need to cook in two batches.

SERVES: 1

NUTRITION: FAT – 21.7G, NET CARBS – 16G, PROTEIN – 68.4G, CALORIES – 573

Ingredients:

- 1 T-bone steak
- ¼ cup of Worcestershire sauce
- ¼ cup of balsamic vinegar
- 1/8 cup of soy sauce
- 1/2 tsp. garlic powder
- 2 tbs. coarse-ground black pepper
- ½ tsp. kosher salt
- ¼ tsp. onion powder

Method:

1 In a medium-sized baking dish, pour the Worcestershire sauce, balsamic vinegar, and soy sauce. Stir together. Add the black pepper, kosher salt, garlic powder, and onion powder and mix together.

2 Place the steak in the dish. Turn over to ensure both sides get coated in the marinated. Cover and place in the refrigerator to marinate for at least 30 minutes, and up to 4 hours.

3 After marinating, let the excess marinade drip from the steak and place on your air fryer's tray.

4 Cook the steak at 400°F for 8 minutes, depending on how done you like your steak. Turn the steaks over halfway through the cooking time. For well-done steaks, cook until the internal temperature (not touching the bone) reaches 160°F. For a medium-rare steak, cook until the internal temperature reaches 140°F.

3-Cheese Grilled Cheese Sandwich

When it comes to cooking cheese in an air fryer, you have to be careful that the cheese is not exposed directly to the heat most of the time. Otherwise, you might find yourself with a dry mess of a sandwich. Luckily, you can take steps to counteract that issue by keeping the cheese contained to the middle of the bread. That said, there's no reason to compromise on taste and flavor when making an air fryer grilled cheese sandwich!

SERVES: 1

NUTRITION: FAT – 42.4G, NET CARBS – 47.6G, PROTEIN – 26.2G, CALORIES – 669

Ingredients:

- 2 slices of ciabatta bread
- 1 tbs. shredded Monterey Jack cheese
- 1 tbs. shredded cheddar cheese
- 1 tbs. shredded Havarti cheese
- 1 tomato (small)
- 1.5 tbs. butter (softened)

Holly M. Adams

Method:

1 Butter both sides of each piece of bread (not just the outside).

2 In a small bowl, mix together the three varieties of cheeses. Place the cheese on one of the pieces of bread, keeping it from the edges of the bread. The cheese will of course melt during the cooking process, but piling it this way will help contain the cheese from spreading out during cooking.

3 Slice the tomato into thin pieces and place a couple of slices on top of the cheese. Cover with the second piece of bread and press down to hold the sandwich together.

4 Put the sandwich on your air fryer's tray and cook at 350°F for about 4 minutes. Flip with a spatula, and cook for another 3 minutes.

Holly M. Adams

SIDES

Bacon-Wrapped Asparagus

Bacon-wrapped asparagus couldn't be easier to cook in your air fryer. You can get your greens while also enjoying the savory flavor of perfectly cooked bacon! Even better, you won't have to worry about the splatter of grease around your stove. It will all be confined to the inside of your air fryer, making it a breeze to clean.

SERVES: 3

NUTRITION: FAT – 18.3G, NET CARBS – 4.3G, PROTEIN – 16.2G, CALORIES – 245

Ingredients:

- 12 asparagus spears
- 6 strips of bacon
- Olive oil spray
- Salt
- Pepper

1 Lay a strip of bacon flat on a cutting board. Place two asparagus spears over the bacon. Then, wrap the bacon tightly around the spears. Wind the bacon so that it covers as much of the stalk as you can.

2 Place the bacon-wrapped spears in your air fryer. Cook at 400°F for approximately 7 minutes, or until the bacon is cooked thoroughly and the asparagus is tender. You do not need to flip the spears, as the bacon will crisp up on both sides. However, you will want to check on the spears as they are cooking to make sure the ends are not burning. If they begin to burn, lightly spray with a small amount of olive oil.

3 Remove the bacon-wrapped spears from the fryer and sprinkle with salt and pepper.

French Fries (Healthier Air Fryer Version!)

Not many people don't love the delicious taste of crispy fries straight from the fryer. This air fryer version eliminates most of the oil people traditionally associate with French fries but retains that crunch that's essential in any tasty French fry.

SERVES: 2

NUTRITION: FAT – 19.8G, NET CARBS – 40.7G, PROTEIN – 5.8G, CALORIES – 350

Ingredients:

- 1 large Russet potato
- Avocado oil spray
- Salt
- Dipping sauces (ketchup, ranch dressing, mayonnaise, etc.)

1 Peel the potato and slice into thin strips about ¼ of an inch thick. Try to make the strips all the same size, as this will help them cook more evenly while in the fryer. Place the strips in a medium sized bowl.

2 Lightly spray the potatoes with the avocado oil spray. Using your hands, toss the potato strips in the oil to ensure all the strips are coated on each side.

3 Place the oiled strips into the air fryer basket, lining them up beside one another, but not letting them touch. You'll likely have to divide them in multiple batches due to the size limitations of most air fryers.

4 Cook the fries at 375°F for around 15 minutes, flipping them halfway. Sprinkle with the desired amount of salt and serve with ketchup, homemade ranch dressing, mayonnaise, etc.

Crisped Parmesan-Zucchini Spears

While French fries in the air fryer are a more heart-healthy alternative to traditionally fried ones, you can go a step further and opt for a side of zucchini spears with your meal. These crisp zucchini spears are just as good served with a burger as fries! You'll get the added health benefits of zucchini, including plenty of folate and potassium.

SERVES: 3

NUTRITION: FAT – 6.5G, NET CARBS – 4.3G, PROTEIN – 10.2G, CALORIES – 108

Ingredients:

- 1 large zucchini (Note: You can use frozen zucchini pieces to make your spears less dry)
- Olive oil spray
- 1/4 cup of grated Parmesan cheese
- Salt
- Pepper

Method:

1. Cut the zucchini into equal-sized spears that are approximately 1/4-inch thick and 4 inches long. Leave the skin on.

2. Place the spears in a medium sized bowl. Spray lightly with olive oil and mix to thoroughly coat the spears with the oil. Sprinkle the grated cheese over the zucchini spears. Press the cheese into the zucchini firmly to help it stick better to the pieces.

3. Put the spears in your air fryer basket in a single layer, leaving enough space for the air from the fryer to circulate around them. Cook at 360°F for about 9 minutes, flipping once halfway through.

4. Once cooked, sprinkle with salt and pepper and serve warm.

Crunchy Broccoli Florets with Sesam

When it comes to health benefits, it's hard to find a green vegetable healthier than broccoli. This hardy vegetable is known for its fiber content, not to mention its high levels of Vitamin C. Cooking vegetables like broccoli in your air fryer means you get the nutritional advantages of the food while limiting the amount of oil you're cooking with.

SERVES: 4

NUTRITION: FAT – 1.7G, NET CARBS – 4.6G, PROTEIN – 1.9G, CALORIES – 37

Ingredients:

- 1 head of broccoli (You can also use frozen broccoli florets for extra moisture)
- 1 tsp. garlic powder
- 1/4 tsp. salt
- 1/4 tsp. white pepper
- 1/2 tsp. onion powder
- 1 tbs. sesame seeds
- 1 tbs. avocado oil

1 Cut the broccoli florets from the head of broccoli, discarding the main stalk. Try to cut the florets into equal-sized pieces, but make sure you don't cut them too small or the broccoli will begin to crumble. Place the broccoli in a large bowl.

2 Drizzle the avocado oil over the broccoli and toss to mix.

3 In a small bowl, mix the garlic powder, onion powder, salt, and white pepper. Sprinkle the seasonings over the broccoli and mix thoroughly, ensuring the seasonings are spread over all the broccoli.

4 Cook the broccoli at 390°F in your air fryer basket for approximately 8 minutes.

5 While the broccoli cooks, heat a medium-sized griddle or frying pan on the stovetop over medium heat. Sprinkle the sesame seeds onto the pan in an even layer. Toast for approximately 10-20 seconds or until they begin to turn a light brown color.

Air-Fried Plantain Chips with Cayenne Pepper

If you've never tried a plantain before, you're missing out. While they resemble bananas in appearance, plantains are less sweet and lend themselves well to savory flavors. These plantain chips are ideal for anyone with a hankering for a quick snack or as a side dish for fish and other meats.

SERVES: 2

NUTRITION: FAT – 1.4G, NET CARBS – 29.8G, PROTEIN – 1.4G, CALORIES – 123

Ingredients:

- 1 large plantain
- 1 tbs. avocado oil
- 1 tsp. cayenne pepper
- ¾ tsp. salt
- ½ tsp. black pepper

Method:

1 Remove the peel from the plantain. Cut each edge of the plantain off and discard. Slice the remaining plantain into 1/4-inch thick pieces. Place the pieces in a large bowl.

2 Add the tablespoon of avocado oil to the plantain pieces and mix to coat all the pieces.

3 Add the cayenne pepper, salt, and black pepper to the bowl and toss to coat.

4 Spread the plantain pieces in a single layer in the air fryer's basket. You may need to cook in multiple batches, depending on the size of your fryer.

5 Cook at 370°F for approximately 10 minutes, or until the plantains are tender.

Brussel Sprouts with Soy Sauce

Brussel sprouts are a controversial vegetable, but when cooked in an air fryer, there isn't much room for debate! These Brussel sprouts will get crispy, and if you use a bit of oil, will retain some of their internal moisture. Paired with a savory soy sauce and honey flavor, you'll want these sprouts to be your main course!

SERVES: 4

NUTRITION: FAT – 4G, NET CARBS – 21.4G, PROTEIN – 5.1G, CALORIES – 125

Ingredients:

- 1 lb. Brussel sprouts
- 1 tbs. olive oil
- 1 tsp. garlic powder
- 1/2 tsp. salt
- 1/2 tsp. pepper
- 1/4 cup of soy sauce
- 2 tbs. honey
- 1 tsp. ginger paste
- 1 tsp. minced garlic
- Sesame seeds (optional)

1 Wash the Brussel sprouts and trim the end (stem) off of them. Remove any browned outer leaves. Carve a small "X" into the core to help them cook evenly.

2 Place the trimmed Brussel sprouts into a bowl. Drizzle the tablespoon of olive oil over them and use a spoon to help coat all of the sprouts.

3 In a separate bowl, mix the garlic powder, salt, and pepper. Pour these seasonings into the bowl with the Brussel sprouts and toss to combine.

4 Arrange the Brussel sprouts in an even layer on your air fryer's pan. Cook at 350°F for about 12 minutes.

5 While the sprouts are cooking, prepare the sauce. In a medium-sized bowl, mix the soy sauce, honey, ginger paste, and minced garlic. Whisk together.

6 Remove the Brussel sprouts from the air fryer (keeping them on the tray). Drizzle the sauce over the Brussel sprouts. Return to the air fryer for an additional minute or two to let the honey thicken slightly. Top with sesame seeds if desired.

Spicy Corn on the Cob

Are you surprised to learn that you can even cook corn on the cob in your air fryer? It's true. Cooking corn is as simple as can be when it comes to using this cooking technique. A staple of summer dinners, corn on the cob that is crisp taste delicious when covered in a slab of butter, salt, and pepper.

SERVES: 4

NUTRITION: FAT – 11G, NET CARBS – 29.2G, PROTEIN – 5.1G, CALORIES – 214

Ingredients:

- 4 cobs of sweet yellow corn
- 1 tbs. vegetable oil
- 2 tbs. butter
- Salt
- Pepper
- 1/4 tsp. chili powder
- 1/2 tsp. Tajin seasoning

Method:

1 Remove the husk and silk from the corn cobs. If wet from washing, dry corn cobs with a paper towel.

2 Lightly coat the cobs with the vegetable oil. You can also use an oil spray if that helps you disperse the oil better. Rub in the oil to make sure all the sides are evenly coated.

3 Place corn cobs in a single layer in the air fryer. Cook at 380°F for 5 minutes. Open the air fryer, turn cobs over using a pair of tongs, and cook for an additional 5 minutes or until the kernels are tender enough to be pierced with a fork.

4 Remove corn from the air fryer and place on a plate. (If you prefer to eat your corn in a less messy manner, stand the corn cobs on end. Carefully slice the kernels from the cob, allowing them to fall onto the place. Discard cobs and continue to Step 5.)

5 Add a ½ tbs. of butter to each cob (or serving of corn kernels). Sprinkle with salt and pepper to suit your preferences. Then, sprinkle the chili powder and Tajin seasoning over the corn, making sure to get all sides. Alternately, you can place the seasonings on another plate and roll the buttered corn cob into the seasoning.

6 Serve warm.

Cheesy Potato Wedges with Sour Cream and Chives

When you need a side to go with your main course, why not veer away from standard French fries and opt for potato wedges instead? Potato wedges are a thicker variant of French fries and add more flavor than traditional fries. This style is sometimes referred to as "steak fries" and their name says it all – they're a filling accompaniment to steak, chicken, or burgers.

SERVES: 6

NUTRITION: FAT – 9.6G, NET CARBS – 12.3G, PROTEIN – 4.3G, CALORIES – 149

Ingredients:

- 2 Russet potatoes (large)
- 1 tbs. olive oil
- 1 tsp. Cajun seasoning
- 1/2 tsp. salt
- 1/2 tsp. pepper
- 1/2 cup of shredded cheddar cheese
- 1/2 cup of sour cream
- 1/4 cup of chives

 Holly M. Adams

Method:

1. Wash and dry the potatoes thoroughly. Leaving the potatoes unpeeled, use a large knife to cut the potatoes in half along the longest part. Slice each half into 6 wedges, and then cut each of those wedges in half. Place the potato wedges in a large bowl.

2. Pour the olive oil over the potato wedges and using your hands, toss the potatoes to make sure the oil covers them completely. Add the Cajun seasoning to the wedges (you can add an extra teaspoon or two of the Cajun seasoning if you like spicy foods). Mix the Cajun seasoning with the wedges.

3. Place the wedges in your air fryer basket. You may need to do a few batches depending on the exact size of the basket.

4. Cook the wedges at 400°F for about 10-15 minutes or until golden brown. Two or three times during the cooking process, carefully remove the basket to shake the wedges around.

5. Remove the wedges from the basket and pour in a serving dish. Cover with the cheddar cheese, dollops of sour cream, and the chives. Sprinkle with salt and pepper as desired.

Eggplant Parmesan with Italian Seasonings

Some people are worried that cooking eggplant is complicated. Fortunately, that's just not the case! Eggplants are a hearty food that's great for vegetarians and meat-eaters alike. When paired with freshly grated Parmesan, it's hard to beat the taste and texture of this often-overlooked ingredient.

SERVES: 4

NUTRITION: FAT – 17.7G, NET CARBS – 46G, PROTEIN – 19.9G, CALORIES – 411

Ingredients:

- 1 small eggplant
- 1 egg (large)
- 1.75 cups of breadcrumbs
- ½ tsp. dried thyme
- ½ tsp. onion powder
- ½ tsp. dried rosemary
- ½ tsp. garlic powder
- 1/2 cup of shredded mozzarella cheese
- ½ cup of grated parmesan cheese
- 1 cup of tomato sauce
- 1 tbs. extra virgin olive oil (optional)
- Olive oil spray
- Salt
- Pepper

Holly M. Adams

1 Wash the eggplant and place on a large cutting board. Cut each end off and discard. Slice the eggplant into ½ inch slices. You do not need to remove the purple outer layer or any of the seeds.

2 In a medium-sized bowl, whisk the egg.

3 In another medium-sized bowl, pour the breadcrumbs, thyme, rosemary, garlic powder, and onion powder. Mix together thoroughly

4 Lightly spray your air fryer's basket with the olive oil spray. Take a slice of the eggplant and dip it into the egg wash. Then place the slice in the breadcrumb mixture. Make sure to push the breadcrumbs firmly into the egg-coated eggplant as you do this, to prevent the crumbs from falling off and burning during the cooking process.

5 Lay the breaded eggplants in the air fryer in a single layer. Cook at 400°F for approximately 3 minutes. Open the air fryer and use a spatula to flip the eggplant slices. Cook for an additional 4 minutes, or until the eggplant has begun to turn a medium golden-brown color. You will likely need to do several batches to prevent overcrowding the air fryer.

6 While the eggplant is cooking, mix the extra virgin olive oil into the cup of tomato sauce if desired. This step is not necessary but adds a bit of richness to the sauce to help the eggplant stay a little moister.

7 In a medium bowl, mix the parmesan and mozzarella cheese together.

8 Spoon a tablespoon or two of the sauce over each of the cooked eggplant slices. Sprinkle with mozzarella-parmesan cheese mixture. Top with a little more salt and pepper if you wish.

9 Place back in the air fryer at 350°F for two or three minutes, or until the mozzarella cheese has begun to turn brown. Serve the eggplant parmesan warm.

Fried Dill Pickle Chips

Never had a fried dill pickle before? You'll want to try this recipe to experience the savory yet tangy taste of this popular snack. Fried dill pickle chips have surged in popularity in recent years, and they're the perfect accompaniment to a sandwich or scoop of chicken or potato salad.

SERVES: 3

NUTRITION: FAT – 0.6G, NET CARBS – 25.6G, PROTEIN – 3.7G, CALORIES – 124

Ingredients:

- 🍽 1 jar of dill pickles (Using thicker-cut slices will keep your chips juicy on the inside)
- 🍽 3/4 cup of flour
- 🍽 1 tsp. garlic powder
- 🍽 1 tbs. dried dill weed
- 🍽 Salt
- 🍽 Pepper
- 🍽 Vegetable oil spray

Method:

1 Lightly spray your air fryer's basket with vegetable oil spray and set aside until ready for use.

2 Drain the jar of dill pickles. In a medium-sized bowl, mix the flour, garlic powder, dill weed, salt, and pepper.

3 Dip each pickle slice into the flour mixture, pressing the flour into the pickle to help it stick better. Lay the pickle slices in an even, single layer in the air fryer basket. Make sure the slices aren't touching one another so that the air can circulate as the chips are cooking in the basket.

4 Cook the pickle chips at 400°F for 5 minutes. Use a long fork or tongs to flip each chip and cook for another 3 minutes. If you like especially crispy pickle chips, you can leave in for another minute or two, but watch them carefully to ensure they don't burn.

5 Dip your pickle chips in ketchup, ranch dressing, or even honey mustard.

Holly M. Adams

Crispy Kale Chips Roasted with Olive Oil

While you typically want to avoid using leafy greens in your air fryer, kale is an exception to this rule. Kale is somewhat hardier and thicker than other types of leafy greens, so it can withstand the intensity of the air fryer. Just make sure to coat each piece well with the olive oil, or you might end up with brittle, dry pieces.

SERVES: 4

NUTRITION: FAT – 13G, NET CARBS – 4.9G, PROTEIN – 10.1G, CALORIES – 168

Ingredients:

- 2 cups of kale
- 2 tbs. olive oil
- 1/2 tsp. garlic powder
- 1/2 tsp. salt
- 1/2 tsp. pepper
- 1/4 cup of parmesan cheese (optional)

Method:

1 Rinse the kale leaves and dry on a cloth. Make sure they are completely dry before using them. Tear the kale leaves into small pieces and place in a large bowl.

2 Drizzle the olive oil over the leaves and toss to coat, making sure that all of the leaves have a good layer of olive oil on them.

3 In a small bowl, mix the garlic powder, salt, and pepper. Sprinkle the seasoning mixture over the chips and toss to evenly coat.

4 Put the kale chips in your air fryer basket and cook at 350°F for about 5 minutes. If adding parmesan cheese, remove the chips after 4 minutes and sprinkle on the parmesan cheese in the last minute of cooking time. Cook until the parmesan cheese melts and the kale chips have crisped.

Holly M. Adams

SNACKS

Crunchy Fried Cauliflower Bites (Spicy!)

When people think of snacking, cauliflower is not always the first thing that comes to mind. However, air fried cauliflower is actually a convenient snacking option that isn't just easy to prepare, but it's delicious as well. Cauliflower is known for its potassium and fiber benefits, so you can feel great knowing you made a healthier choice when it comes to snacking! Using frozen cauliflower is also fine and even adds a bit of extra moisture to the dish.

SERVES: 3

NUTRITION: FAT – 9.8G, NET CARBS – 41G, PROTEIN – 12.9G, CALORIES – 292

Ingredients:

- 1 head of cauliflower (medium)
- 1/2 cup of flour
- 2 eggs (large)
- 1/2 cup of breadcrumbs
- 1 tbs. chili powder
- 1 tsp. cayenne pepper
- 1/2 tsp. chipotle powder
- 1 tbs. olive oil
- Salt
- Pepper

Method:

1 Lightly cover the air fryer's basket with oil to prevent the cauliflower from sticking. Set the basket aside until needed.

2 Rinse the cauliflower and cut into even-sized florets. Make sure to leave some of the "stem" on the cauliflower so that the pieces don't crumble.

3 In a large bowl, mix the flour, breadcrumbs, chili powder, cayenne pepper, chipotle powder, salt, and pepper.

4 In another bowl, whisk the two eggs.

5 Dip each cauliflower floret into the egg wash and then into the breadcrumb mixture, pushing the crumbs into the egg mixtures to help them stick.

6 Place the cauliflower in a single layer in the air fryer. Cook at 370°F for approximately 5 minutes. Flip the cauliflower using a fork, and then cook another 5 minutes, or until the cauliflower has begun to turn brown. Do not overcook.

7 These cauliflower bites pair well with any creamy dip, as the cream will help to balance out the bites' spiciness. For a less spicy variation, leave out the chipotle powder.

Sweet-Heat Potato Crisps

Have you made the switch to sweet potatoes yet? Plain potatoes are a thing of the past. Sweet potatoes, as their name suggests, have a more sugary flavor than typical potatoes. Not only do they taste decadent, but they're also loaded with nutrients that make choosing to cook with them an even smarter choice!

SERVES: 4

NUTRITION: FAT – 3.7G, NET CARBS – 21.4G, PROTEIN – 1.2G, CALORIES – 121

Ingredients:

- 🍽 2 sweet potatoes (large)
- 🍽 1 tsp. salt
- 🍽 ¼ tsp. black pepper
- 🍽 1 tsp. chili powder
- 🍽 1 tbs. extra virgin olive oil

Holly M. Adams

1 Wash potatoes and then dry them with a paper or cloth towel. You can choose to peel them if you like, but sweet potatoes crisps are equally delicious with their skins still on.

2 Slice the sweet potatoes in half lengthwise. Then cut each half into 1/4-inch "half-moon" shapes.

3 Drizzle the olive oil over the potatoes and toss to coat evenly with the oil.

4 Lay the potato pieces in your air fryer's basket in a single layer, making sure none of them touch one another. Be sure to leave enough space to allow for air circulation.

5 Cook the crisps at 370°F for around 12 minutes, using tongs or a long fork to flip them halfway through the cooking process. Cook until they begin to brown and turn crispy.

6 While they cook, mix the salt, pepper, and chili powder in a small bowl. Sprinkle the seasoning mix on top of the crisps after they're done cooking. If desired, serve with dipping sauces of your choice.

Tortilla Chips

Do you love nibbling on a salty snack in between meals? These tortilla chips are the ideal solution for munching on a quick snack without adding tons of extra calories from excessive amounts of oil. Tortilla chips are simple to make and serve as a convenient base ingredient for dishes like nachos, chilaquiles, and more!

SERVES: 4

NUTRITION: FAT – 2.1G, NET CARBS – 32.2G, PROTEIN – 4.1G, CALORIES – 157

Ingredients:

- 🍽 12 corn tortillas
- 🍽 Avocado oil spray
- 🍽 Salt

1 Place two corn tortillas onto a cutting board. Stack them on top of each other. Using a large, sharp knife, cut the tortillas into 6 equal pieces. You can do this by cutting in half, and then cutting three triangles from each of the halves.

2 Put the pieces into your air fryer's basket. Use the avocado oil spray to lightly coat the tortilla pieces with oil. Shake the basket to ensure all the chips get coated.

3 Cook the tortilla chips at 350°F for approximately 6 minutes. Check them in the last minute or two to keep an eye on them to prevent burning.

4 Serve with salsa or top with ground beef, shredded cheddar cheese, and sour cream for a late-night nacho snack.

Sliced Mushrooms with Garlic-Parmesan

Looking for a snack that has plenty of flavor without tons of calories? Try this mushroom recipe and see how air fried mushrooms can pack punch with less.

SERVES: 2

NUTRITION: FAT – 12.2G, NET CARBS – 5.2G, PROTEIN – 19.3G, CALORIES – 196

Ingredients:

- 1 basket baby portobella mushrooms
- 2 cloves garlic
- ½ cup of grated parmesan cheese
- Avocado oil spray
- Salt
- Pepper

1 Slice the mushrooms into 1/4-inch pieces and place in a large bowl.

2 Remove the outer layer from the garlic cloves. Using the side of a knife, carefully crush the garlic cloves to help release some of the flavor. Add the garlic to the mushrooms.

3 Lightly coat the mushrooms and garlic cloves with avocado oil and toss to evenly coat.

4 Place the mushrooms and garlic in a single layer in the air fryer. Cover with parmesan cheese.

5 Cook at 350°F for 10 minutes. Check on them halfway to adjust cooking time if necessary. Garlic can burn in the air fryer, so be sure to remove the cloves if they begin to get too crispy.

6 Sprinkle with salt and pepper according to your preferences.

Air Fryer Blooming-Style Onion

Blooming onions are a popular appetizer in restaurants around the country, and with an air fryer, it's never been easier to cook one at home. While the average air fryer's size can make cooking for several people at once difficult, a blooming onion helps navigate this challenge by cooking a quick snack that's easy to duplicate.

SERVES: 4

NUTRITION: FAT – 2.6G, NET CARBS – 27.8G, PROTEIN – 6.5G, CALORIES – 161

Ingredients:

- 1 yellow onion
- 1 cup of flour
- 2 eggs
- ½ tsp. onion powder
- ¼ tsp. cayenne pepper
- 1 tsp. garlic powder
- Avocado oil spray
- 1 tsp salt
- 1 tsp. pepper

Holly M. Adams

Method:

1 Peel the onion and using a sharp knife, carefully cut the onion almost in half, stopping just before reaching the onion's base. With each of the cuts you make, you'll want to make sure you don't cut completely through the base. (If you do so, you can still use the onion pieces, but they will not be attached.) Make another similar cut in the opposite direction (perpendicular). Finally, make two diagonal cuts in an "X" shape across the cuts you've already made.

2 Carefully separate each of the onion pieces apart from each other. Set the onion aside.

3 In a large bowl, mix the flour, garlic powder, onion powder, cayenne pepper, salt, and pepper.

4 In another large bowl, whisk the two eggs together. Dip the whole onion into the egg mixture. You'll want to make sure the onion is completely coated in the egg mixture, so you can use a spoon at this step, or you can even place the onion in an empty bowl and pour the egg wash directly over it.

5 Then, pour the flour mixture over the egg-covered onion. Use your fingers to press in the flour to ensure it sticks while cooking. Spray with avocado oil.

6 Place the onion in your air fryer and cook at 350°F for about 20 minutes. Check on the onion every few minutes, spraying with more oil as necessary to prevent burning.

7 The onion is cooked once you are able to pierce one of the "petals" easily with a fork. Serve with ketchup, ranch, mayonnaise, etc.

Holly M. Adams

Golden Tater Tots with Cheddar Cheese

When you need a snack with a bit of crunch, a bit of salt, and plenty of cheese, this tater tot recipe is for you. Whether you have a midnight snack craving or just want something to tide you over until dinner, cooking these tater tots is not only easy but quick, too.

SERVES: 4

NUTRITION: FAT – 1.4G, NET CARBS – 18.1G, PROTEIN – 3.3G, CALORIES – 96

Ingredients:

- 🍽 2 Russet potatoes (medium)
- 🍽 ½ yellow onion
- 🍽 1 egg
- 🍽 Salt
- 🍽 Pepper
- 🍽 Vegetable oil spray

1 Wash, dry, and peel the potatoes. Using a grater, grate the potatoes over a large bowl. Be careful at this step, as the moisture in the potatoes can make them slippery.

2 Finely dice the onion and add to the bowl of potatoes. Mix well.

3 In a small bowl, whisk the egg. Drizzle the egg over the potato-onion mixture. Mix the egg in.

4 Set out a baking pan or plate. Using your hands, mold the mixture into small balls, about 1.5 inches round. Carefully shape them into rounded rectangles and place them on the dish. Continue until you've used up all of the potato mix.

5 Spray the tots with vegetable oil. Turn over on the pan and spray the undersides.

6 Place in your air fryer basket and cook at 400°F for 15 minutes. Shake the basket gently halfway through the cooking process.

7 Once the tots have turned golden brown, remove from the air fryer and sprinkle with salt and pepper. Serve with ketchup or another dip of your choice.

Paprika-Cumin Fried Chickpeas

Fried chickpeas are a common street food snack in many parts of the world. With an air fryer, you get the delicious crispness of the peas without all of the added fat. When looking for chickpeas in the store, be aware that they are also called garbanzo beans.

SERVES: 6

NUTRITION: FAT – 4.5 G, NET CARBS – 45.2G, PROTEIN – 13.7G, CALORIES – 268

Ingredients:

- 1 15.5 oz. can of chickpeas
- ¼ cup of flour
- 1 tbs. cumin
- 1 tsp. paprika
- ½ tsp. salt
- ½ tsp. black pepper
- Vegetable oil spray

1 Drain the can of chickpeas. Using your hands or a paper towel, carefully remove the outer layer of the chickpeas and discard. This step is optional, but it will help your chickpeas have a bit more flavor and will help the seasoning stick better.

2 In a large bowl, mix the flour, cumin, paprika, salt, and pepper. Pour the chickpeas into the mixture. Using your hands, toss the chickpeas to coat them lightly with the flour.

3 Place the chickpeas in your air fryer basket and spray with the vegetable oil. Gently shake the basket and spray a little more to make sure all of them are covered.

4 Cook in your air fryer at 400°F for approximately 10 minutes. Shake the basket halfway through cooking to help the chickpeas brown evenly.

Italian-Style Meatballs

Are you looking for a snack that's a little more filling than just carbs? These meatballs with Italian seasoning are a bit more substantial than some of the other snacks found in this recipe book. You'll stave off your hunger pangs while enjoying the savory flavor of these meatballs.

SERVES: 4

NUTRITION: FAT – 7.3G, NET CARBS – 9.9G, PROTEIN – 35.5G, CALORIES – 257

Ingredients:

- 1 lb. ground beef (75-85% lean)
- ½ yellow onion
- ¼ cup of flour
- ½ tsp. onion powder
- 1 tsp. sage
- 1 tsp. rosemary
- 1 tsp. parsley
- 1 tsp. thyme
- ½ tsp. garlic powder
- ½ tsp. salt
- ½ tsp. black pepper
- 2 tbs. Worcestershire sauce

1 Place the ground beef in a large bowl. Using a spatula or a spoon, break up the beef into small pieces.

2 Cut the onion into very fine pieces and add to the bowl of beef. Mix well.

3 In a medium-sized bowl, add the flour, sage, rosemary, parsley, thyme, garlic powder, onion powder, salt, and black pepper. Pour the seasoning mixture over the beef and mix in. Then add the two tablespoons of Worcestershire sauce and mix in thoroughly.

4 Using your hands, form small balls (approximately 2 inches in diameter) from the meat mixture.

5 Place the balls in a single layer in your air fryer. You do not need to coat these with oil.

6 Cook at 350°F. After 5 minutes, open the air fryer lid and using tongs, turn the meatballs over so the underside can cook. Cook for another 5 minutes or until the meatballs are cooked to an internal temperature of 160°F and are golden brown.

Spicy Cheddar Cheese Sausage Balls

If you're looking for a spicier alternative to the recipe above, why not try cooking these spicy cheddar cheese sausage balls? They offer a little extra heat and make a great appetizer for any event with family and friends. They're perfect for giving guests something to munch on while waiting for the main course to finish cooking.

SERVES: 6

NUTRITION: FAT – 31.1G, NET CARBS – 9.1G, PROTEIN – 23G, CALORIES – 412

Ingredients:

- 1 lb. ground sausage
- 1.5 cups of shredded cheddar cheese
- ½ cup of flour
- 1 tbs. red pepper flakes
- ½ tsp. cayenne pepper
- ½ tsp. salt
- 1 tsp. black pepper
- 1 tsp. Tabasco sauce (2 tsp. for extra spice)

1 Place the ground sausage in a large bowl. Use a fork or spatula to break into smaller pieces. Add 1 cup of the cheddar cheese (reserving the other $1/2$ cup for later) and mix together.

2 In a separate bowl, mix the flour, red pepper flakes, cayenne pepper, salt, and pepper. Sprinkle over the sausage mixture and work into the mix, combining thoroughly.

3 Add a teaspoon of Tabasco sauce (or two if you like a lot of heat) and mix well.

4 Use your hands to shape the sausage into small bowls about 2 inches in diameter.

5 Place the sausage balls in a single layer in your air fryer tray. Cook at 350°F for about 10 minutes, turning them once to help them cook evenly. Once they've browned and reached an inside temperate of 160°F, top with the remaining cheddar cheese and serve warm.

Stuffed Jalapeno Peppers with Avocado

A classic snack in many restaurants around the nation are stuffed jalapeno peppers. Sometimes known as jalapeno poppers, this dish is a wonderful combination of some of the most mouth-watering foods out there: cream cheese, bacon, and spicy jalapeno peppers. The air fryer can help transform those raw leftover jalapenos into their own dish! If you want to keep the heat to a minimum, look for jalapenos that are solid green (without grey streaks), as these ones are milder in flavor.

SERVES: 4

NUTRITION: FAT – 36.3G, NET CARBS – 8.4G, PROTEIN – 17.8G, CALORIES – 424

Ingredients:

- 8 jalapeno peppers
- 8 strips of thick-cut bacon
- ½ cup of cream cheese
- ½ tsp. garlic powder
- 1 tsp. chili powder
- 1 ripe avocado
- Avocado oil spray
- Salt
- Pepper

1 While wearing gloves, cut the jalapeno peppers in half lengthwise. Take out the seeds and the inner ribs and discard.

2 In a small bowl, mix the cream cheese with the garlic powder and chili powder.

3 Use a small spoon to scoop the cream cheese mixture into the insides of the jalapeno halves.

4 Wrap each jalapeno half with a piece of bacon. If you're not able to wind the bacon around the entire jalapeno, spritz with a bit of the avocado oil spray to keep the jalapenos moisturized while cooking in the fryer.

5 Place the jalapeno halves on your air fryer's tray. Leave a bit of room around each of them so that they don't touch while they're cooking.

6 Cook the jalapeno peppers at 350°F for about 10 minutes, or until the bacon has cooked completely through and the jalapenos are tender.

7 Remove from the air fryer. Slice the avocado into thin slivers and top each jalapeno pepper with a slice or two.

Holly M. Adams

DESSERTS

Banana Smores with Walnuts

If you have children or are simply still a child at heart, these air fryer banana smores are sure to put a smile on your face. While people don't always think of desserts when they think of air fryers, this equipment can actually cook up quite a few tasty dishes to end your meal!

SERVES: 4

NUTRITION: FAT – 21.8G, NET CARBS – 48.7G, PROTEIN – 5.8G, CALORIES – 398

Ingredients:

- 🍽 4 bananas (large)
- 🍽 1 tbs. butter
- 🍽 2 graham crackers
- 🍽 1/2 cup of mini marshmallows
- 🍽 1/2 cup of mini chocolate chips
- 🍽 3/4 cup of whipped cream
- 🍽 1/4 cup of chopped walnuts

1. Unpeel the bananas and cut in half lengthwise and place the halves in a large bowl.

2. Melt the tablespoon of butter in a small bowl. Allow the butter to cool until safe to handle, and then pour the butter over the bananas. Using a baker's brush, brush the butter over the bananas.

3. Place the bananas in a single layer in your air fryer. Cook at 350°F for about 3 minutes, and then flip with a spatula. Cook for another 2 or 3 minutes, or until the bananas have begun to brown and soften.

4. While the bananas are roasting, crush the 2 graham crackers in a small bowl. You can do this by using the back of a large spoon. Alternately, you can place the whole graham crackers in a plastic bag and crush with your hand.

5. Remove the bananas and place on a plate. Top with the marshmallows, chocolate chips, whipped cream, and walnuts.

Sweet Cinnamon Monkey Bread

Monkey bread isn't just a cute name. It's an addictive treat that virtually everyone loves! This recipe is great for a summer night when you feel like staying in with friends or family and sharing a flavorful dessert. Monkey bread is best eaten when warm, so plan accordingly!

SERVES: 10

NUTRITION: FAT – 22.3G, NET CARBS – 54.4G, PROTEIN – 5.1G, CALORIES – 428

Ingredients:

- 2 cans of biscuit dough (flaky is best)
- 1 tbs. vegetable oil
- 1 cup of butter (unsalted)
- 2 tbs. cinnamon + another 2 tbs. cinnamon
- 1 tsp. ground cloves
- ½ cup of brown sugar
- ½ cup of white sugar
- 1 tsp. nutmeg

Holly M. Adams

1. Grease the inner pot of your air fryer with a tablespoon of oil. Set aside.

2. Open the cans of biscuit dough and mix together to form a large ball of dough. Place in a large bowl. Add two tablespoons of the cinnamon and the white sugar. Mix well to combine.

3. Place the biscuit mixture into the prepared air fryer pot.

4. Melt the cup of butter and pour into a separate, medium-sized bowl. Add the remaining two tablespoons of cinnamon, cloves, brown sugar, and nutmeg to the butter and whisk together.

5. Pour the butter mixture over the biscuit dough.

6. Bake at 320 °F for around 15 minutes or until the inside of the bread has set.

Easy French Toast with Cinnamon-Sugar Topping

French toast doesn't always have to be a breakfast dish. In fact, we think it actually serves better as a dessert! This recipe pulls together the sweetness of bread, butter, cinnamon, and sugar, resulting in a purely delightful way to end an evening meal.

SERVES: 6

NUTRITION: FAT – 17.5G, NET CARBS – 31.2G, PROTEIN – 4.8G, CALORIES – 293

Ingredients:

- 6 pieces of Texas toast-style bread
- 1 egg
- 1/2 cup of milk
- 1/2 cup of butter
- 1/4 cup of white sugar
- 2 tbs. cinnamon

Holly M. Adams

1 Whisk the egg, cinnamon, and milk together in a large bowl.

2 A piece at a time, dip the bread into the egg, cinnamon, and milk mixture and place on a large plate or a baking sheet.

3 Place the toast pieces in a single layer in the air fryer. You'll need to do multiple batches due to the size constraints of the fryer.

4 Cook at 350 °F for approximately 8 minutes, flipping the toast pieces halfway through.

5 Melt the butter on the stovetop over low heat. Mix in the white sugar and stir to combine. Pour over the French toast and sprinkle with extra cinnamon if desired.

Donut Holes with Light Lemon Icing

Donut holes are a delightful treat any time of day. Whether you want to eat a few with your morning cup of coffee or with your afternoon tea, donut holes have just the right amount of sweetness to offset a warm beverage. These lemon-icing donut holes are a good pairing with Earl Grey tea or a strong cup of Columbian roast coffee.

SERVES: 6

NUTRITION: FAT – 17.2G, NET CARBS – 62.7G, PROTEIN – 7.1G, CALORIES – 431

Ingredients:

- 2 cups of flour
- ¼ cup of white sugar
- 4 tbs. oil + 1 tbs. for greasing
- 1 packet of instant yeast
- 1 cup of milk
- 1 cup of powdered sugar
- 2 tbs. butter
- 1 tsp. vanilla extract
- 2 tsp. lemon juice
- 1 egg (medium)

Holly M. Adams

1 Grease the air fryer basket with 1 tbs. oil. Set aside.

2 In a large bowl, mix the flour and white sugar together.

3 In a separate bowl, whisk the milk and yeast together. Leave the mixture to rest for 5 minutes to allow the yeast to activate.

4 Mix the milk and yeast with the egg and the remaining 4 tbs. oil. Whisk well until combined thoroughly.

5 Pour the liquid ingredients into the dry ones and mix until just combined.

6 Using your hands, mold a bit of the dough into a small ball, about 1.5 inches in diameter. As you form the donut holes, place them in the air fryer basket.

7 Bake in the air fryer at 350°F for about 7 minutes. Gently shake the air fryer basket a few times while they cook, as this helps to make them brown evenly.

8 While the donut holes bake, prepare the icing. Pour the powdered sugar into a large bowl. Melt the two tablespoons of butter in a separate bowl in the microwave, and then pour on top of the powdered sugar.

9 Mix well. Add the vanilla extract and lemon juice. If you prefer your icing thicker, add more powdered sugar. If you want it a bit thinner, you can add a little extra lemon juice.

10 Let the donut holes cool completely (approximately 1 hour). Once cool, drizzle the lemon icing over the donut holes.

Holly M. Adams

Pecan-Cinnamon Rolls

Another classic example of dessert as breakfast, pecan-cinnamon rolls are enjoyable no matter what time of day it is. These rolls blend together the fragrant cinnamon with just enough sugar. You can cover these cinnamon rolls with a layer of white icing if you want to add an extra level of decadence to this dessert. The pecans in this dish give a bit of crunch in every bite.

SERVES: 8

NUTRITION: FAT – 16.4G, NET CARBS – 46.8G, PROTEIN – 6.9G, CALORIES – 352

Ingredients:

- 2 cups of flour
- ¹/₂ cup of white sugar + ¹/₄ cup
- 1 egg
- ³/₄ cup of milk
- 1 tsp. vanilla extract
- 2 tbs. cinnamon powder + 2 tbs.
- ¹/₂ cup of pecans (roughly chopped)
- Vegetable oil spray

1 In a large bowl, mix the flour, $1/2$ cup of white sugar, and 2 tbs. of the cinnamon powder.

2 In another, medium-sized bowl, whisk the egg, milk, and vanilla extract together.

3 Pour the egg mixture into the flour blend and mix thoroughly.

4 On a surface lightly dusted with flour, roll out the dough mixture. Form a large square about 12" by 12".

5 In a small bowl, mix the remaining $1/4$ cup of white sugar, the remaining 2 tbs. of cinnamon, and the chopped pecans. Evenly sprinkle this cinnamon-pecan mixture of the square of dough so that the entire dough piece is covered with cinnamon and sugar.

6 Starting from the bottom, gently roll up the square so that it forms a large "log".

7 Use a sharp knife to cut the dough log into 12 pieces about one-inch thick. You should see the cinnamon swirl in the cross section of the cut piece.

8 Lightly spray your air fryer's tray with the vegetable oil. Place the cinnamon roll slices flat on the tray about an inch apart (leaving room to expand).

9 Bake at 350°F for about 12 minutes. If desired, top with additional pecans and cover with icing.

Not-So-Traditional Chocolate-Chip Cookie

It comes as a surprise to many people that you can make cookies in the air fryer. What's an even bigger surprise is that you can make a giant cookie in one! Some people refer to it as a "pizookie." Whatever you want to call it, just know that it is amazing. Be sure to pour a large glass of milk to go along with it!

SERVES: 8

NUTRITION: FAT – 12.9G, NET CARBS – 58.4G, PROTEIN – 5.2G, CALORIES – 367

Ingredients:

- 1 3/4 cups of flour
- 4 tbs. butter (softened)
- 1 egg (medium)
- 1 cup of white sugar
- 1 cup of chocolate chips
- 1 tsp. vanilla extract
- Vegetable oil spray

1 Pour the flour into a large bowl. Mix in the white sugar.

2 In a separate medium bowl, combine the melted butter, vanilla extract, and the egg. Blend with the flour and sugar. The dough will be soft and somewhat thick.

3 Add in the chocolate chips. For a less sweet cookie, you can reduce the amount of chocolate chips.

4 Spray the vegetable oil on your air fryer pan (including the sides). Put the cookie dough into the pan and spread it throughout the pan. Smooth down any bumps on the top with the back of your spoon.

5 Bake the cookie at 350°F for around 8 minutes. After 8 minutes, check to see whether the cookie has fully set and is a slight golden-brown color. Remember that the heat from the cookie will continue to cook it for just a few moments after you remove it, and that it will harden a bit as it cools, so be sure not to overcook it.

Disclaimer

This book contains opinions and ideas of the author and is meant to teach the reader informative and helpful knowledge while due care should be taken by the user in the application of the information provided. The instructions and strategies are possibly not right for every reader and there is no guarantee that they work for everyone. Using this book and implementing the information/recipes therein contained is explicitly your own responsibility and risk. This work with all its contents, does not guarantee correctness, completion, quality or correctness of the provided information. Misinformation or misprints cannot be completely eliminated.

Printed in Great Britain
by Amazon

86230524R00064